Dinner Party Ideas

Diana Stanley

Dinner Party Ideas
by Diana Stanley

ISBN 978-1-926917-16-0

Printed in the United States of America

Images on pages 50 and 60 © Getty Images

Neither the author nor the publisher assumes any responsibility for the use or misuse of information contained in this book.

TABLE OF CONTENT

INTRODUCTION

Hosting a successful dinner party doesn't have to be stressful or painful. In fact, it should be fun and something that both you and your guests can enjoy. Planning and hosting a dinner party can be fun and easy to pull off if you know how to go about it.

One of the best things about planning a dinner party is that the style you choose can be entirely up to you. You can plan a menu as elaborate or as simple as you would like. In this guide we will walk you through the basic steps of planning a successful dinner party, including everything that should be taken care of in advance, handling the guest list, centerpieces for the table, how to set the table and much more.

Remember, you do not have to a professional chef or party planner in order to entertain like one. We will walk you through the steps of planning the entire event as well as provide tips on hiring others to help you execute a wonderful dinner party. Whether you are planning a luncheon for an intimate group of friends or a holiday open house, you will find everything you need to know about planning a successful dinner party in this guide.

Ready to begin planning your first dinner party?

Let's get started!

GETTING STARTED

Dinner Party Planning Basics

Planning a dinner party can be stressful, especially considering the many things that must be considered. From the invitations to the food to the music to the ambience and the entertainment, every element of the event must be skillfully managed in order to plan the ideal dinner party. Understanding how to approach the process of planning a dinner party and when to handle the planning of each item can help you to pull off the perfect dinner party.

The most important thing you can know about planning the perfect party is to always plan in advance. This will help to eliminate many of the snags and problems that you might otherwise encounter. Planning in advance will also ensure that you have more time during the party to actually enjoy yourself and your guests without worrying about last minute details.

An important element to consider when you are planning any type of dinner party is why you are planning the event. Is it for a holiday, office party, birthday or simply an excuse for friends and family to get together? Whatever the reason, it is a good idea to have a clear vision of why you are hosting the event so that you can convey this intent to the people invited to the party.

You should also consider what the objective of the party will be. What type of party will you host? This can be extremely important and relevant to many other details related to the party. For instance, if you plan to host a themed party, then the decorations and perhaps even the food will need to be tied in with that overall theme. A themed party need not be expensive with a little thought and creativity. For instance, you could plan a party around a single recipe or invite everyone over to celebrate the big game. Do you and your friends enjoy a good bottle of wine? What about hosting a wine tasting party? As you can see there are many different options.

Of course, you must also consider who you will invite to your party. This is crucial in planning the event. Will everyone invited to the party know one another? Are you inviting only close friends? Family Co-workers? Business associates? Whatever the case may be, it is important to consider whether everyone there will be acquainted with one another.

You will also need to consider the total number of people you are planning to invite, their particular likes and dislikes and what they have in common. Understanding the different variables of your guests will help you to plan a party that will be enjoyed by everyone.

The choice of venue is also important. Location cannot be stressed enough. There are many different factors that should be considered when selecting a location for any dinner party. In many cases you may choose to host the event in your own home but you might also choose to host it elsewhere if your place is too small or you are inviting a large number of people. Ideally, you should make sure there is plenty of space for everyone to be comfortable, adequate lavatory facilities, access to food and beverages and space for everyone sit/stand comfortably.

You should also consider whether you have enough space for parking and whether there is space for guests to leave their vehicles if they should need to take a taxi home.

If you do choose to rent a venue for your dinner party, consider the following questions:

- Does it have food and beverage facilities?
- If so, will they provide the room free if you use their services?
- Are there adequate lavatory facilities? Are they wheelchair accessible?
- Is there an outdoor area available for smoking?
- At what time will you be able to gain access to the facility? At what time must you leave?
- Will you be responsible for cleaning after the event?
- Are there adequate electrical outlets?
- What is the capacity of the venue?
- Is security available?

You should also consider the date and time for your dinner party. When you choose to host your party can impact not only where you have your party but may also impact who you invite as well.

Consider the following time lines:

- Will the party fall on a holiday?
- Will the start time for the party accommodate your guests' schedules?

Invitations and Guest Lists

One of the most important parts of the planning process is the guest list. You need to make sure that you send out invitations early enough to ensure you have a confirmed guest list well in advance of the event. Be sure to include any pertinent details in the invitations such as the time, place, etc.

When planning your party, be sure to include the interests of the people you plan to invite to the party as you plan elements such as the food, music, entertainment, etc. For instance, if you plan to invite any vegetarians to the event, be sure to include some appropriate dishes on the menu. Ideally, you should plan to invite between six and twelve guests for a dinner party, with six being the ideal number. Try to balance out the guest list between both new and old friends as well as people from a variety of different aspects of your life in order to keep the conversation varied.

Once you have determined who you would like to invite to your dinner party, you will need to give the guests ample advance notice; ideally two weeks before the party date. Keep in mind that the formality of the invitation you use will dictate the overall tone for the event. For example, a phone call or email would suggest a casual get together while a custom or handwritten invitation signals a more special event.

Dinner Party Guest List

Name	Telephone Number	Invitation Sent	RSVP
			Yes/No
			Yes/No
			Yes/No
			Yes/No
			Yes/No
			Yes/No
			Yes/No
			Yes/No
			Yes/No
			Yes/No
			Yes/No
			Yes/No

Sample Dinner Party Invitation Wording

Example 1

The honor of your presence is requested
at Location, Address, on Date
For Dinner and Cocktails at Time
Name of Hosts
RSVP Information

Example 2

Please be our guest for Dinner and Dancing
on Date
at Time
Location
RSVP

Example 3

Join us for the Annual Neighborhood Block Party
Date
Time
Location
Please bring a covered dish.
RSVP by Date to Contact

Example 4

Food, Friends, Fun
You are invited for an evening of good food and
conversation at the home of Name
Date
Time
RSVP by Date

Example 6

It's that time of year for our Family Holiday
Gathering. This year it is at the home of Name
on Date and Time. Be sure to bring your favorite
holiday dish.

Dinner Party Styles

There are three basic types and styles of dinner
parties; buffet, cocktail and sit-down dinner.

Buffet Dinner

A buffet that is festive and well thought out can
be fun as well as easy. It allows you to get away
from the kitchen and spend more time with your
guests. You can plan something as simple and
casual as various types of pasta with salad and
garlic bread or even a standing rib roast with all

of the trimmings. There are actually two different types of buffets. One is a lap service buffet in which guests will eat either while standing or while seated in chairs or on a sofa. This style makes it easy to mingle and talk while still nibbling. It works well for small parties and receptions in smaller venues. It's also a good choice for a night of movie watching or a casual evening.

A sit-down buffet is more suitable for an elaborate occasion such as a family holiday or small dinner party.

Formal Sit-Down Dinner

A formal sit down dinner is typically served in courses. Make sure you invite your guests at least half an hour before you plan to serve the meal to allow for a cocktail or before-dinner drinks period.

Informal Sit-Down Dinner

An informal sit-down dinner may or may not be served in courses as you wish. The food can be more casual with this type of dinner as well.

Brunch

Brunch is a choice that makes it possible to easily fit it into a sit-down dinner or a buffet. It is also a low maintenance way of entertaining. Try to keep things low-key.

Cocktail Party

A cocktail party typically lasts around two hours and is a good choice when you are limited on resources and time. Cocktails can be as elaborate or as simple as your time and resources will allow. During a cocktail party it is easy for guests to nibble on a few appetizers, enjoy a drink or two and then move on. You can serve a cocktail party either on a buffet or by passing a tray. If you choose the tray pass method keep in mind you will need a waiter to pass through the guests with the appetizers, in addition to help in the kitchen to keep platters filled.

It is best to offer an assortment of appetizers that include meat or seafood as well as cheeses and vegetables. You should plan to serve at least six different appetizers for a group of ten people or less. For up to twenty people, offer ten different appetizers and for a group of up to forty people, plan on a dozen different appetizers.

Keep in mind that guests will typically eat between eight and twelve pieces of appetizers during a basic two hour cocktail party, so make sure you have plenty on hand.

Laying out a Buffet

If you choose to serve a buffet meal or serve appetizers buffet style, it is important to make sure that you have everything laid out in a logical order. This means that plates should be placed at one end of the table and food in the middle with cutlery and napkins at the other end of the table. Food should be set out with main dishes placed front and center, vegetables to the side, salads on the opposite side and breads and desserts placed toward the back.

Setting the Tone with Music

The right ambience is always important when planning a dinner party. The best way to handle this is to make sure that you have set up the music in advance of the party by organizing your CDs or creating a special playlist on your iPod. Regardless of what type of music you choose make sure the volume will not detract from the conversation. When properly selected dinner music can help to create an atmosphere that is soothing and calming. Selecting the dinner music is something that can be done well in advance of the actual event, freeing up your time on the day of the event for other activities.

In choosing the type of music you will have for your event, try to select music that will remain in the background while guests are at the table. This will allow conversation to take center stage and not the music. Soft classical instrumental music is always an excellent choice for a dinner party.

Setting the Scene

No matter what kind of dinner party you will be hosting, it is important to always make sure the scene is set. This can be part of the fun of hosting a dinner party because it allows you to use your imagination and incorporate a number of things, including napkin rings, napkins, candles, place settings, centerpieces, flowers, etc.

If you have not chosen a specific theme with which to work, you might think about the time of year and what is seasonally available. For instance, if your party is during the fall you could use beautiful fall flowers and small pumpkins. During the winter, it is easy to work with rich and vibrant colors such as reds and greens.

Games and Activities

Prior to your event, decide whether you will incorporate any games or activities into your dinner party. This is certainly not a necessity as lively conversation can be enough entertainment. If you are not certain how well your guests will get along; however, some games or activities can be welcome. Below are some games and activities that can help to break the ice and help everyone to feel more comfortable with one another.

Message Under a Plate

This is a very simple and easy game that can

quickly liven things up at a dinner party. All that is needed is a pen, small slips of paper and some imagination. Begin by writing out a different phrase on different pieces of paper. Place one strip or paper under each of the guest's plates. The phrases should be usable but unique. Prior to dinner ask everyone to read the paper under their plate but not aloud. Then ask them to use their phrase as naturally as possible in conversation. The goal is for the other guests to figure out when another guest is using their phrase. If they are able to use the phrase without anyone detect it they win the game.

Famous Name Game

This activity can easily be played at the dinner table as well or you can choose to play it before dinner or after dinner. This is a wonderful way to keep the conversation going if it becomes quiet. You do not need any supplies. In this game, each guest is required to say the name of a celebrity. The first guest will begin with a name. Any name can be used. The guest to the right of the first guest must then say another name but the name must begin with the first letter in the last name of the celebrity the previous guest listed. The game will continue in the same manner around the table. No name can be listed more than once. If a guest does make a mistake by pausing, re-using a name, not having an answer, speaks out of turn or misses their turn they can be required to then say or do something silly to keep things lively.

The Memory Game

This is another relatively simple and easy game that can be played either around the table or before or after the party. The only thing you need for this game is a good memory. Begin by having one guest say something they are going to bring to a party such as "I went to a party and brought a bottle of wine." The next guest must then add another item to the previous guest's item. For example, "I went to a party and I brought a bottle of wine and a bouquet of flowers." The game will continue with each guest naming off all of the prior items and then adding one of their own.

Conversation Starters

Starting a conversation at your party should not be difficult or stressful. It is perfectly natural to talk about your day but there are many topics which can be thought provoking and help to stimulate conversation when needed, such as the following:

- What would you like to accomplish this year?
- What subject do you wish you knew more about?
- Tell us something you think everyone should know about you.
- What are you most proud of?
- What surprised you most about today?
- If you could choose a new name for yourself,

what would it be?
- What book are you reading right now?
- What is your favorite summer/fall activity?

The Menu

When planning the menu it is important to keep a few factors in mind including the tastes of your guests as well as your own experience in the kitchen, the number of ingredients needed and the complexity of the recipes you select. You should decide on the number of courses that will be served in advance, including whether you will have hors d'oeuvres available when guests arrive and whether you will serve a soup or salad course or dessert. For the most part, three to four courses is a good number for a dinner party.

Remember as well that if this is to be your first dinner party, it is not the best time to begin experimenting with recipes that are complicated or new. Try to use recipes that will make it possible for most of the work to be done in advance so that you will have plenty of time to enjoy your guests during the actual dinner party. Good choices include fish or meat dishes that are marinated in advance. You might also consider dishes that can be served at room temperature such as salads and certain vegetables. When possible, try to only select one main course that will require attention.

Remember to keep color in mind when selecting the food you will serve at your party. It can be surprisingly easy to choose foods that are all tasty but the same color when presented together. Try to select dishes that will have contrasting colors. This can be easily done through a selection of various vegetables.

It is also a good idea to consider any important food issues your guests may have. While it is impossible to cater to the dislikes of every guest, it is important to check with guests when inviting them regarding any serious food issues they may have such as allergies, whether they are on a strict eating regimen, whether they are diabetic, etc. Even if one or more guests do have a serious food issue it is usually fairly easy to work around them. For instance, if a guest has a serious seafood allergy, simply do not serve any seafood. You will find that most guests will be quite happy to suggest ways in which you can handle any issues they may have without disrupting the entire menu.

To make matters easier for yourself, do try to select a menu with as many dishes that can be made ahead of time as possible if you are going to prepare the meal yourself. This is particularly true if you are not that experienced in the kitchen. Preparing make ahead dishes can greatly help to reduce the amount of stress you experience on the actual day of the event and give you more time to enjoy your guests. In addition, it can help you to avoid any last minute problems if preparation should take longer than you might have originally thought. This will also give you plenty of time for cleaning up after cooking. If there should be a disaster, such as if you burn something, you will have ample time for coming up with a change in plans; something that is difficult to do if you are preparing the meal on t he day of the party.

It is also a good idea to restrict any special recipes to just one or two dishes. Not every dish needs to be special. Instead, select one or two items that you will really focus upon. The remainder can be tasty but relatively simple.

You may also find that it is a good idea to select a day prior to the party to prepare your meal during a time when you do not have as much pressure. This will allow you to freeze the meal and then all you will need to do is heat it on the day of the party.

Also keep in mind that there is no strict rule which says you must personally prepare everything you serve at your dinner party. If you choose to prepare the main course, you could very easily purchase an appetizer and dessert. You could also order the entire meal from a restaurant and then serve it on your best dishes. The main thing is to make sure your guests feel comfortable and the party flows well, not for you to spend the entire time working away in the kitchen.

When planning the shopping for your menu, keep in mind that it can often be helpful to plan two shopping trips; one larger one well in advance of the event and a smaller trip one to two days before the dinner party. If you do choose to do two smaller trips, plan to pick up any perishables on the second trip as well as anything that might not have been available during the first trip.

Choosing Wine

Wine, when properly chosen, can be a wonderful addition to any dinner party; however, the process of choosing the right wine to complement certain dishes is something that can leave many people confused. This is often because there are so many questions associated with choosing the right wine such as what color goes with what food, how much you should pay for a good wine, what wine matches which food, etc.

The first thing to keep in mind is that you need not become confused over the process of choosing wine and you need not be a wine expert to make good selections. Also, you shouldn't be afraid to take advice by consulting your local wine store for advice about matching food and wine.

Even if you do not ask for advice; however, there are some basic guidelines that can be kept in mind to help you choose a good wine for your dinner party. There are actually four elements that should be considered when selecting wine.

They are:

- Weight
- Flavor
- Color
- Cost

Weight

The weight of a wine simply refers to the alcohol content. Light means that the wine is between 8 and 10% alcohol. Medium refers to a wine that is about 10.5% and 12% alcohol while a full bodied wine is 12.5% to 16% alcohol.

Flavor

Flavor refers to both the texture and flavor of the dish. Sweet dishes should be matched to wines that have a sweet flavor while dishes that are heavier and more robust should be matched to wines that are more acidic. You may find that the wines at your local wine store are rated from 0 to 10. 0 refers to a wine that is very dry or non-sweet while 10 is very sweet. If you are not certain about the rating of a wine, you can always ask the wine staff.

Most people typically match the flavor of the wine to the strongest dish they will be serving. Therefore, if you are going to be serving a dish that is highly flavored, you should select the wine based on the strongest flavor of that dish. Without doing this, the dish could overpower the wine.

Color

One thing to keep in mind when it comes to the color of wine is that champagne will complement anything you might choose to serve. Beyond this, most people typically select white wine with lighter weight or dishes that are paler in color and red wine for heavier dishes.

Cost

How much should you spend on wine for your dinner party? The most important thing is that you and your guests enjoy the wine, not how much you spend. So, instead of focusing on the cost of the wine try instead to focus on the other factors such as color and weight rather than the cost.

Sample Dinner Party Menus

Appetizers/ Hors D'oeuvres

If you will not have a lot of time, plan to set of appetizers that can be self-served.

Soup and Salad

Cold soups such as vichyssoise or gazpacho can be prepared in advance and simply retrieved from the fridge for serving. Salads can also be prepared in advance but make sure you do not dress it until the last moment.

Main Course

Remember to plan something simple that will not require a lot of your time and attention.

Dessert Course

To save time, make sure you do not plan anything complicated. You might even consider buying a dessert.

Sample Menu 1

Appetizer
Roasted garlic bread, shrimp cocktail

Second Course
Gazpacho
Main Course
Smoked salad, grilled corn on the cob, tomato and mozzarella salad

Dessert
Grilled pineapple

Sample Menu 2

First Course
Shrimp cheese spread and crackers

Second Course
Mixed greens and sourdough bread

Main Course
Pork roast, roasted potatoes, parmesan asparagus

Dessert
Lemon sorbet

Sample Menu 3

First Course
Wine along with bite size assorted fruit such as grapes, apples, cranberries and pears.

Second Course
Pork roast, garlic mashed potatoes, herbed green beans

Third Course
Pumpkin pie, apple streudel or cranberry crisp

Fourth Course
After dinner coffee

Sample Menu 4 - Mexican Fiesta

First Course
Margaritas, assorted dips and chips

Second Course
Tortilla soup

Third Course
Carnitas, refried beans, rice

Fourth Course
Mexican coffee and flan

Sample Menu 5

First Course
Crab appetizers

Second Course
Seared lamb chops with Dijon mustard
Roasted potatoes
Spinach salad

Third Course
Mini-apple pies with vanilla ice cream

Sample Menu 6

First Course
Portabella mushroom crostini

Second Course
Caesar salad

Third Course
Vichyssoise

Fourth Course
Lemon Sorbet

Fifth Course
Cornish game hens served over wild rice

Sixth Course
Chocolate mousse cake

Sample Menu 7

First Course
Walnut, arugula and gorgonzola crostini
Fresh shrimp on ice with cocktail sauce

Second Course
Baby artichokes with mustard dipping sauce

Third Course
Arugula Salad

Fourth Course
Grapefruit and mint sorbet

Fifth Course
Prime rib with Au Jus
Small new red potatoes
Snow peas and carrots

Sixth Course
Chocolate ice cream

Seventh Course
Lattes

Sample Menu 8

First Course
Brie cheese and assorted crackers

Second Course
Italian salad-fresh tomato slice, mozzarella cheese
and fresh basil

Third Course
Zucchini soup

Fourth Course
Chicken breasts stuffed with Boursin cheese

Fifth Course
Coffee with kahlua

Buffet Menu Ideas

Soup Buffet

- Wild rice chowder
- Gazpacho
- Chilled cucumber soup
- Vichyssoise
- Split pea soup
- A variety of breads and crackers

Salad Buffet

- Assorted greens
- Chicken salad
- Macaroni salad
- Cobb salad
- Crudite platter
- Variety of dressings

Italian Buffet

- Antipasto platter
- Caesar salad with dressing and croutons
- Chicken cacciatore
- Orecchiette pasta
- Penne pasta with tomato basil sauce
- Assorted focaccias
- Tiramisu

Menu Planning Form

Appetizers	
Soups/Salads	
Main Dish(s)	
Side Dish(s)	
Dessert(s)	
Wine and Drinks	

TIMEFRAME AND PLANNING

As previously mentioned, one of the best things you can do to make sure that your party is successful is to plan as much in advance as possible. The following timeline will help you to keep everything running on track.

Planning Checklist

Two to Three Weeks Before the Party
- Decide on the reason for the party
- Decide on the style and/or theme for the party
- Decide on the date, time and place.
- Make a budget
- Create guest list.
- Extend invitations
- Decide on table settings, including the centerpiece
- Check tablecloths, napkins, dishes and flatware to determine if there is anything missing or that needs to be replaced.
- Plan the menu. Write down all of the necessary ingredients and create shopping list.
- Buy any staple items needed.
- Check pantry and check off items you already have.

2-3 Days Before the Party

- Purchase food and flowers
- Purchase wine and any other drinks
- Clean house so only last minute touchups will be left on the day of the party.

- Decide on what you will wear on the day of the party.
- Make any dishes that can be prepared in advance.

1-2 Days Before the Party

- Make sure that you have finished all of your food shopping at least one day ahead of the event. You should never leave everything for the actual day of the party. This will also allow you ample time to run out for any last minute items you may have forgotten.
- Arrange centerpiece(s).
- Set the table (one day before).
- Make any food items that can be prepared 24 hours in advance.
- Select dinner music.
- Lay out dessert and coffee dishes and supplies

Several Hours Before the Party

- Make sure you have finished up any necessary cleaning well in advance of the start time of the party.
- Prepare any food that can be done in the morning
- Lay out serving dishes and utensils
- Lay out pre-dinner appetizers
- If you have not already arranged flowers, this should be done now.
- Set the table.

- Lay out any needed serving dishes.
- If you will be serving buffet style, make sure it is set up.

One Hour Before the Party

- Make sure you are dressed and ready to greet guests at least one hour before the party is to begin.
- Prepare any beverages you will be serving and make sure that any necessary garnishes are prepared. Also, make sure glasses and napkins are set out.
- Set the lighting. Remember that the lighting should be bright enough for everyone to see but not so bright that there is no ambience or atmosphere.
- Take care of any necessary prep work now to save time for later on.
- Consider starting the main course or entrée if it will take more than twenty minutes in the oven so that you can then keep it warm until you are ready to serve.

Just Prior to Guests Arriving

- Set out hors d'oeuvres
- Start music.
- Open and/or decant wine

At the Party

- If you have skillfully handled the planning up to this point, you should be able to relax and enjoy the presence of your guests.

As Guests Arrive

- Remember to introduce guests who may not know one another.
- Attempt to highlight what guests who may not know one another well have in common as conversation starters.
- • If you need to return to the kitchen, ask a friend to keep an eye on things and let you know if you are needed.

During the Party

- Make a point to regularly check on things to see if drinks or appetizers need to be replenished.

At the End of the Party

- If it seems that everyone is having too good of a time to leave but you need to end the evening, try adjusting the lighting or turning off the music to discretely signal the end of the party.
- Always make sure your guests have a safe ride home. If anyone has over-indulged - call a taxi.

Supply Checklist

The following checklist will help to make sure you have everything you need on the day of your dinner party.

Cocktail Hour

- Assortment of cheeses
- Assortment of crackers
- Cheese knives
- Cheese twists
- Crudités
- Cocktail glasses (lowball and martini)
- Flowers (décor)
- Gin
- Grapes, pears, sliced apples, etc.
- Hummus
- Ice bucket, ice, ice tongs or scoop
- Lemons
- Limes
- Mixed nuts
- Napkins (allow 2 for each guest if using paper)
- Olives
- Platters
- Small canapé plates
- Soda
- Tonic (plan 1 bottle for every 3 guests)
- Toothpicks
- Vodka
- Water glass (1 for every guest)
- Wine (1 bottle for every 2-3 guests)
- Wine glass (1 for each guest)

For Dinner

- Candles
- Centerpiece
- Napkins
- Place cards
- Tablecloth
- Coffee and assortment of tea bags
- Cream and sugar

For Serving

- Bread board or bread basket
- Bread plates
- Coffee cups, saucers and spoons
- Coffee/tea service set
- Decanter
- Dessert plates
- Dinner plates
- Salad plates
- Serving platters
- Silverware
- Water goblets
- Water pitcher
- Wine coasters
- Wine glasses

Miscellaneous

- Coat rack or a separate room to place coats
- A place to put umbrellas and boots
- Additional toilet tissue for powder room
- Pretty guest soaps for powder room

AVOIDING MISTAKES AND PROBLEMS

Keep in mind that even if you do have a problem or make a mistake with your dinner party, it does not have to mean that the entire event is a disaster. Even so, understanding some of the most common mistakes and how to avoid them can help you to have a far less stressful dinner party and enjoy yourself more.

Perhaps one of the biggest and most common mistakes that many people make when planning a dinner party is getting carried away. This often takes the form of planning a menu that is too large and complicated. While there is nothing wrong with planning one dish that is somewhat complicated, you should not plan multiple dishes or items that are complicated. For instance, if your main dish will be somewhat complex make sure your appetizers and pre-dinner cocktails are simple. The same should go for side dishes and the dessert.

You will probably find that matters are much easier if you assign seating. This can be easily accomplished by simply using place cards on the table so there is no question about where everyone should sit. Some general guidelines to follow when it comes to seating include:

• Never have couples sit next to one another
• Never have family members sit next to one another
• Never have people who do not get along sit next to one another

These general guidelines will ensure that conversation is lively and varied while helping to avoid possible disagreements.

In addition, make sure you do not leave too much to do at the last minute. Planning in advance can help to avoid this common problem. Try making a to do list, working backwards from the time guests will arrive to make sure you have everything worked out well before your guests will begin arriving.

Overall, remember to follow these guidelines and you can avoid many of the most common mistakes associated with planning a dinner party:

- Make sure your dinner party plan and menu are simple
- Stick with the plan and avoid last minute changes and/or additions
- Plan your seating in advance
- Do not leave too much to do at the last minute

SETTING YOUR TABLE

Setting the table for any event is often considered to be stressful for many people. In actuality, it is not that complex. There are a few simple rules and guidelines that should be adhered to and once you learn those the process can enjoyed instead of dreaded.

One of the most important things to keep in mind when it comes to the table setting is that you are essentially creating a design for the table and as is the case with any design there are certain elements that are necessary in order to create the whole design. In the case of a table setting, those parts include china, glassware, china and linen. If you choose to use them, you may also include decorations that will fit into the overall theme for the event.

Table Sizes

One important element you will need to consider when planning your dinner party is how everyone will be seated. The size table(s) you will need will be dictated by the number of people you will invite to your party. The following guidelines can assist you in determining how many and what size tables you need for your party. These guidelines are based on seating up to ten people:

- A rectangular 6' by 30" table will seat up to 8 people
- A rectangular 8' by 30" table will seat up to 10 people

- A 48" round table will seat between 6 and 8 people
- A 60" round table will seat between 8 and 10 people

Table Coverings

The table covering or table cloth forms the background for the entire table setting. You can choose white or a color that matches a theme, but regardless the table covering you use should be wrinkle free and clean. Keep in mind that regardless of how well a tablecloth is washed, there are bound to be creases in the folds which can be removed through ironing or steaming.

You can also use placemats whether your event is formal or casual. Placemats can be used along with tablecloths or instead of tablecloths. Generally, placemats are used for breakfast and lunch and a tablecloth is used for dinner. If you do choose to use a placemat, make sure a mat is positioned beneath each dish.

In the restaurant business, the space that is set aside for each person at the table is known as a cover. The cover includes the linen as well as the silver, china and glassware that will be used by each guest. You should allow between twenty and twenty-four inches of table space for each cover at a formal table setting. This will ensure there is no bumping of elbows and that no one feels crowded.

If you like you may also wish to include a silence cloth on your table. A silence cloth is merely a second table cloth that is placed beneath the tablecloth that will be actually seen in order to absorb any noise from the dishes as they are placed on the table. Since the silence cloth will not actually be seen you can use almost anything from a plain tablecloth to a bed sheet.

When placing the tablecloth on the table, keep in mind that it is best to actually unfold the cloth on the table rather than open the cloth and then throw it over the table. Tossing the cloth on the table tends to crumple it. Make sure the center of the tablecloth forms a line through the center of the table so that the four corners have an equal distance from the floor. The tablecloth should never hang less than nine inches below the edge of the table on all sides. The centerpiece should always be placed in the center of the table.

Centerpieces

There are certainly many different options that are available for centerpiece choices. You can use anything from a live plan to a dish of fruit to a vase of cut flowers. The actual style of the centerpiece should vary based on the formality of the event. Regardless, you should make sure that the centerpiece is not so high that it creates an obstruction and guests are forced to lean around it in order to converse with others across the table.

Table Settings

If you are not familiar with what is involved in a proper table setting, a table setting diagram may be helpful. If you choose to use a placemat, it should be placed at the edge of the table. The china, napkin and silver should be placed one inch from the edge of the placemat.

The large dinner plate should be positioned in the center of the placemat or approximately two inches from the edge of the table if only a tablecloth is used.

When setting a basic or informal table, there is really no need to use more than three pieces of silver on each side of the plate. If you should need additional silver, you can always bring it in as each course is served. Also, keep in mind that silverware items should not be placed in the table setting if there is no food to be eaten with it. All flatware should be placed on the table in the order it will be used with the first utensils situated farther away from the plate. This allows guests to work their way inward as they progress with each course.

Also, if you are going to serve coffee and it will be served away from the table, such as in the living room, you also do not need to worry about placing a spoon on the table unless it will be needed for another food item. Silver which is to be used with the left hand should be placed to the left of the plate and that which is to be used with the right hand will be placed to the right of the plate.

Therefore, forks should be placed to the left and knives and spoons should be placed to the right. The only exception to this rule is the seafood cocktail fork, which is placed to the right since it is used with the right hand unless the guest is left-handed. The sharp side of the knife should always be turned inward toward the plate.

The water glass should be placed to the right at the tip of the dinner knife. During a luncheon or dinner you may also substitute goblets. If you are going to serve wine, the wine glass should be placed to the right of the water glass. The glasses should be arranged so that they form a diagonal line to the spoons. In the event you are going to serve more than one type of wine, such as a wine with dinner and then a dessert wine, the glass for the first wine that will be served should be placed closer to the guest's right hand.

It is entirely up to you as to whether you use bread and butter plates. They are more commonly used in semi-formal luncheons and dinner parties rather than formal dinner as they offer space for olive pits, relishes and bread. If you are planning a casual party with a food that may come with toothpicks or have some type of waste you may wish to provide a bread and butter plate for the refuse.

Napkins

The napkin can be positioned in one of two ways. At a dinner party or luncheon where a first course will be served after the guests have been seated, you can fold the napkin into a rectangle and place it across the plate. It is also acceptable to place the napkin to the left of the forks. The open corner of the napkin may be positioned either away from or toward the plate; but whatever you decide, make sure all of the napkins are positioned in the same way.

You certainly do not need to learn any fancy methods for folding a napkin, but if you wish there are two very simple and effective techniques which can be used.

The Fan

Begin by opening each napkin fully and laying it flat on the table. Fold the napkin back and forth in the same way you would a fan. Press the napkin down so that all of the creases are sharp. Now, fold the long rectangle in half and place the center in an empty glass. Open both ends of the napkin that are sticking out of the glass so they form a fan shape. The glass can then be positioned in the original placement or in the center of the plate.

The Triangle

The triangle is even easier than the fan. Open the napkin flat and fold one corner on top of the opposite corner. Take one of the remaining corners and fold it over the opposite. Fold these corners on top of the other corners and crease them. Now, take the corner that used to the be center and place it in an empty glass.

Salad Plates

If salad is to be served, the salad place should be positioned to the left of the bread and butter plate. When individual salt and pepper shakers are used they should be placed at the top of the plate. Keep in mind that you do not need to use individual salt and pepper shakers, but they do allow guest to continue conversation uninterrupted without the need to ask anyone to pass the shaker.

In a formal table setting, there will typically be more silver items and the table setting will be slightly more complex. In most instances, the more formal the occasion, the more courses will be served and that means more flatware items will be needed.

A different set of utensils should be used for each course that is served. For instance, a salad fork, a dinner fork and a dessert fork. A dinner knife, a bread knife, etc. There are some dishes that may require special utensils, such as oysters. These utensils can be served as the food is presented, but they are typically placed on the table in the order of the course serving.

Special Circumstances

If you know that you are going to have left-handed diners, make an effort to seat them at the end of a long table, especially if you are going to have a formal table setting.

Keep in mind that if you know that two people who have extremely divergent political opinions or two people who are known for not getting along, you should not seat them near one another. Lively conversation and debate is one thing; loud arguments are another.

DINNER PARTY ETIQUETTE

When hosting a dinner party, it is always important to know some basic rules of etiquette. While you should never correct your guests, understanding a few basic rules can help to ensure things operate a bit more smoothly.

Welcoming and Greeting Guests

Try to make an effort to go to the door and greet each guest as they arrive. If you are not able to do this and must have someone else answer the door, at least make sure you make a point to seek out that guest and personally welcome them as soon as possible.

Try to have your foyer prepared in advance to handle things efficiently by deciding where coats and wraps will be placed and where guests can play purses, gloves, etc. You might also wish to have a mirror in the entryway so that guests can quickly pat down wind-blown hair. Other niceties include a place for wet footwear and umbrellas.

In most instances, there will be about thirty minutes to an hour between the arrival go guests and the time when dinner is served. If a guest has still not arrived when you are ready to begin serving, you should not delay dinner more than fifteen minutes to ensure that other guests are served on time. When the latecomer does arrive, invite them to join everyone at the table during whatever course is currently being served. If you are on the main course, you do not need to rush about and give them the first course.

If you have invited guests who may not be acquainted with everyone, plan ahead to introduce everyone and provide a conversation starter so they can begin chatting. For example, "This is Paul, he just move here this year." Or "Jacob, I'd like you to meet Mary. She is also interested in foreign films."

These types of introductions will provide a natural conversation starter and make everyone more comfortable while also allowing you to slip away to the kitchen if necessary.

Handling Hostess/Host Gifts

In some cases, a guest may bring a gift of chocolates, flowers or wine to a dinner party. You should be prepared to receive such gifts graciously if this happens. You can do this by having a vase and scissors handy if you are presented with flowers or a candy dish for setting out the chocolates. One of the most frequent questions that many people have is whether they should serve wine when it is presented as a hostess gift. This is entirely up to you. The wine is provided as a gift, which means that you do not need to serve it if you would rather not.

It could be that the wine simply does not go with your menu and if that is the case you can politely thank the guest and say that you will certainly enjoy the wine at the next meal you prepare.

Keep in mind; however, that sometimes it can be better to be sensitive to the sensitivity of the guest rather than observing strict protocol and wine guidelines. If you sense that your guest might be offended if you do not serve the wine they brought, you can always go ahead and set it out.

Drinks and Appetizers

Make sure you have planned ahead by setting out ice, glasses and any other supplies or items you may need. If you are hosting on your own, you might ask a guest to assist you in serving the first round of drinks as well as taking charge of refills and serving latecomers if you need to slip into the kitchen for a few moments.

Set out napkins and plates for appetizers. While not all guests will use them it is still a good idea to have them available for those who prefer them. You should also have an empty dish available for disposing of shrimp shells, toothpicks, etc.

Seating Guests

You should plan in advance for the seating of the guests at the table. Remember that it is customary to separate couples when seating them at the table in order to keep the conversation lively and varied. Remember to give your guests a few minutes of warning in advance of serving the meal. This will provide them time to slip away to the powder room or finish a drink.

Basic Eating Etiquette

Everyone should be seated and served before beginning to eat. A courteous hostess may instruct guests to go ahead and begin eating. Remember that it is a good idea to pace your eating so that you do not finish too far ahead of others or lag too far behind.

Bread should be broken into pieces and then buttered rather than buttered all at once.

The napkin should be unfolded and placed on the lap. When finished eating, the napkin should be placed loosely on the table rather than on the plate.

Once the main course has been finished, all dishes and condiments should be removed from the table. Dishes may remain on the table after dessert while everyone talks and enjoys after dinner drinks or coffee/tea. The serving of coffee/tea signals that the formal portion of the evening has ended. At this point guests may feel free to leave or they may linger if the host/hostess encourages them do so.

Winding Down the Evening

As evening begins to wind down, you may choose to invite guests to liver over their coffee or after dinner drinks in the living room or begin to send some subtle signals that the evening is coming to an end. You can do this by turning off the music or beginning on the dishes. Remember to see all of your guests to the door and thank them for coming.

Keeping a Dinner Party Journal

Following any party, it is always a good idea to keep a journal about what worked well and what could be improved upon for next time. If you plan to invite the same guests to a future event you might also write down their preferences and any special issues they might have for future reference. All of this information can be quite handy when planning your next dinner party. In addition, it is a good idea to write down what you wore and what you served so you won't repeat it with the same guests.

Other books by Psylon Press:

100% Blonde Jokes
R. Cristi
ISBN 978-0-9866004-1-8

Choosing a Dog Breed Guide
Eric Nolah
ISBN 978-0-9866004-5-6

Best Pictures Of Paris
Christian Radulescu
ISBN 978-0-9866004-8-7

Best Gift Ideas For Women
Taylor Timms
ISBN 978-0-9866004-4-9

Top Bikini Pictures
Taylor Timms
ISBN 978-0-9866426-3-0

Cross Tattoos
Johnny Karp
ISBN 978-0-9866426-4-7

Beautiful Breasts Pictures
Taylor Timms
ISBN 978-1-926917-01-6

For more books please visit:

www.psylonpress.com

www.ingramcontent.com/pod-product-compliance
Lightning Source LLC
Chambersburg PA
CBHW070940280326
41934CB00009B/1949